DACHAU SERMONS

Martin and Else Niemöller with their twelve-year-old son

MARTIN NIEMÖLLER

DACHAU SERMONS

Translated by

Robert H. Pfeiffer

Harvard Divinity School

2190

LATIMER HOUSE LIMITED

33 LUDGATE HILL, LONDON, E.C.4

Printed and bound in Great Britain by Purnell and Sons, Ltd.
Paulton, Somerset, for

LATIMER HOUSE LIMITED
33 LUDGATE HILL, LONDON, E.C.4

First published in Great Britain, 1947

PREFACE

A Dutch cabinet minister, two Norwegian shippers, a British major from the Indian army, a Yugoslavian diplomat, and a Macedonian journalist constituted the small congregation for which, for the first time after seven and a half years, I conducted a religious service. It was on Christmas Eve in 1944, during post arrest in the Dachau concentration camp. Since all six members of the congregation spoke tolerably good German, their understanding did not present great difficulties. Indeed, we sang our German chorals with a zest and joy to be found in few congregations of our homeland. Our congregation, moreover, was almost as rich in denominations as in nationalities: Calvinists, Lutherans, Anglicans, and Greek Orthodox found themselves together here—nearly all isolated individuals who were cut off and separated from their religious communities as much as from their families and friends. What else was left to us than to put into practice now, as well as we understood it, the *una sancta*, the one Holy Church, and to gather together around God's word? Nay, what else was left to us than also to celebrate together our Lord's Supper? Indeed we did it, and all of us rejoiced with all our hearts in the communion that united us as disciples of the same Teacher and Saviour.

To whosoever would criticize or even condemn this, I can only reply: "If you had been in our situation, confined for years alone without church services, without pastoral care, awaiting day after day for years the liberation or the end, depending for years upon yourself and your pitiful spiritual poverty, then you also would have wandered

5

without fail to Cell 34 and you would have not excluded yourself."

Our place of worship was an ordinary cell which my three Roman Catholic brother colleagues—with whom I was imprisoned during the last four years—had arranged as a chapel in order to celebrate there their daily Mass. It contained an altar table with a crucifix and candles. If someone should go into it today, he could not possibly believe that nine persons not only found room in it, but even celebrated divine services and the Lord's Supper; for later a German married couple joined us seven.

How it happened that we were allowed to celebrate these services is difficult to say. During all the long years it had been forbidden, because we "special prisoners" were not to come in contact with one another. Shortly before Christmas, 1944, permission was suddenly granted when the Dutch royal minister van Dyck requested it, and after that we were permitted to come together every four weeks, and for the holidays there was even a special easement: until our departure from Dachau the time amounted to six vacation hours!

Today I publish the sermons preached at that time; first of all, in order to salute thus my fellow prisoners of the last days at Dachau, but also to show clearly that, amidst the horrors of those days, the Gospel remained alive for us as the power of God. It remains even now our only hope!

MARTIN NIEMÖLLER.

Leoni (Lake Starnberg, Bavaria).

I

CHRISTMAS EVE, 1944

Fear not: for, behold, I bring you good tidings of great joy,
which shall be to all people. For unto you is born this day in the
city of David a Saviour, which is Christ the Lord. And this shall
be a sign unto you: Ye shall find the babe wrapped in swaddling
clothes, lying in a manger.

Luke 2: 10–12

WHEN Christmas must be celebrated in captivity it is
naturally a rather dismal affair. Ordinarily we human
beings are really satisfied only when the holidays, as one
says, "have finally been happily endured again." And this
is readily understood. There is no feast in the course of
the year that moves us so deeply as Christmas, that brings
back so many cherished and intimate memories, that
awakens in us such strong and deep longings for what has
been taken from us!

Thus it happens that in these holidays we feel somewhat
uncertain about ourselves and actually fear continuously
that we may lose control over ourselves. Bitterness in
bearing the burden laid upon us and revolt against our lot
are then particularly close to us. We must strive with
innumerable contending feelings in our breast. And so it
finally happens that we are really glad when the average
daily routine again enfolds us and when the stormy waves
of the emotions, which make us restless and uneasy,
gradually subside again.

Under such circumstances there remains little chance for
the joy of the heart, as we knew it formerly in the Christmas
days and which used to make our souls spacious, luminous,

7

and grateful. We are now indeed a "people that walked in darkness," as the prophets said (Isaiah 9: 2), men who are tossed back and forth between fear and hope and who finally can find nothing better to do than to let things take their course.

But now the ancient proclamation sounds in our ears, those Christmas glad tidings with the angel's announcement to the shepherds in the fields, that moving story of a babe in the manger who would bring to all people joy and salvation. Centuries have drawn comfort, joy, and hope from it; but today it looks almost as if the era of grace was finished, as if all this was merely an echoing sound which our ears still perceive, but which is no longer strong and powerful enough really to set human hearts in motion. If we ask the reason for this, however, we obtain a simple, but significant answer: man has fallen into the habit of living his life without God. My dear friends, I do not wish to be misunderstood. I do not mean the people who call themselves "godless," and for certain scientific, philosophical, or political reasons assert, "There is no God"—people with whom we cannot be classed. I mean decidedly ourselves, who are assembled here, who have not yet discontinued the practice of opening and closing the course of our days with prayer. But God often seems to us to be so infinitely far away that we think He is not concerned with our planet. It does in fact really seem as if He had left this earth to its own devices, in order that mankind might at last destroy it completely. And from this notion it is but a narrow step to the distrustful question, "How could God be concerned with me, a small, miserable, little man, in a time when hundreds of thousands, and millions, perish dismally? Is that not utterly senseless and paradoxical?" The result of such thoughts, which actually force themselves upon us at this time, is that unconsciously we exclude the thought of God from what happens to us day by day, that we see only the human beings and the terrestrial conditions and base on them, according to circumstances, either our hopes or our fears. This is the situation which I have in mind when I say "to live without God", it prevents us from drawing from the Christmas story such comfort, joy, and hope as our fathers did.

Precisely in this plight of the heart the glad tidings of Christmas will bring us help, if only we hear the message properly, and believe it as the word which the living God speaks unto us and which we shall meditate for a moment.

There, then, lies the babe in the manger. Innumerable poets have sung his praises, numberless painters have pictured him, and since the days of our own childhood we see him thus through our inner eye, crowned with a nimbus and transfigured with the romantic radiance which art and the poetry of the human spirit have poured upon that scene in the stable of Bethlehem.

The reality of the gospel message ignores all this fictitious magic. In the tidings imparted to the shepherds only a two-fold "sign" is named for them and for us, i.e., two matters which are significant for this child and his identification: this babe is wrapped in swaddling clothes and lying in a manger. That is all. And what does this tell us? First of all, the child that lies there wrapped in swaddling clothes is no less feeble and helpless than any other babe born into this world. The mother must care for him lest he perish, must wrap him in swaddling clothes lest he freeze to death, must nourish him lest he die of hunger. So the swaddling clothes are a characteristic sign and presage for the life of the man of whom it was said on a later day: "He saved others; himself he cannot save" (Matthew 27: 42). In the second place, the manger likewise is no mere pictorial feature for the enhancement of the poetry of Christmas; it is again a sign, a sign of the homelessness of this babe:

"there was no room for them in the inn." The manger also is an omen, for the babe was to grow into the man who was forced to say of himself, "The foxes have holes, and the birds of the air have nests; but the Son of man hath not where to lay his head" (Matthew 8: 20). These are the two signs given to the shepherds, and to us also.

But if we now look deeper and ask what the human helplessness and earthly homelessness of the infant Jesus can tell us, then the tidings of great joy begin precisely here: God, the eternally wealthy and almighty God, enters into the most extreme human poverty imaginable. No man is so weak and helpless that God does not come to him in Jesus Christ, right in the midst of our human need; and no man is so forsaken and homeless in this world that God does not seek him, in the midst of our human distress.

Here the situation is therefore not as in the man-made religions. These require that we human beings set out to go to a distant deity, throned in its majesty above us in unattainable heights, on which we must laboriously climb —but without ever reaching the goal because our strength is simply not adequate. Here, conversely, God comes down to us and cares for us; and He does not single out the strong and good, in order to abandon to himself and to his fate the feeble and ill. Here, out of the swaddling clothes and the manger, comes this call unto us: "Come unto me, all ye that labour and are heavy laden, and I will give you rest" (Matthew 11: 28). Here takes place what the Apostle Paul comfortingly proclaims to us: "For ye know the grace of our Lord Jesus Christ, that, though he was rich, yet for your sakes he became poor" (II Corinthians 8: 9).

This is what is so singularly peculiar in the Christian message of salvation, which tells us, "You need not go to search for God; you should not imagine that He is far from you and is not concerned with what crushes you! He is here and is close to you in the man who, as a babe

wrapped in swaddling clothes, was lying in the manger.
All your need is so far from being alien to him that on
the contrary he gave himself freely in order to bear it with
you." Whoever can grasp this in faith is not forsaken in
prison and in death; for in the worst darkness he may say,
"Thou art with me; thy rod and thy staff they comfort
me" (Psalm 23: 4).

My dear friends, on this Christmas feast let us seek, in
the babe of Bethlehem, the one who came to us in order
to bear with us everything that weighs heavily upon us.
Then we will undoubtedly become aware of the great joy
that is announced to us; and out of the brilliance that sur-
rounded the shepherds a shining ray will fall into our
darkness. This child is called "Emmanuel, which being
interpreted is, God with us" (Matthew 1: 23). Yea, God
Himself has built a bridge from Himself to us! A dawn
from on high has visited us!

We have thus considered a single phase of the Christmas
message, and it may seem that in this manner the essential
has been said. But there is still another phase, and in the
end it is even more important for us. For sure, the signs
—swaddling clothes and manger—remain loyal to the man
after the child has outgrown them. He goes on his way,
onward into the depths of mankind: he becomes an itinerant
preacher, followed by the common people while great
men and scholars face him with explicit scepticism, if they
consent to notice him at all. He becomes that peculiar kind
of saint who associates with publicans and sinners, with
harlots and lepers. He becomes at last the "man of sorrows,"
betrayed by his own disciple, understood by none of his
friends, and even deserted by God's hand—his earthly life
ended on the cross (and that means on the gallows). "See,
what a man!" His whole life was a path of grief and woe,
from the manger to a grave which was not even his

property. Such is the life of this child, as it unfolds before our eyes.

But God has placed his own superscription on this life; He sends us this message about this child: "Unto you is born this day . . . a Saviour, which is Christ the Lord" (Luke 2: 11). Here more than comfort is at stake, as God inclines toward us; here salvation, deliverance from mortal need and danger are involved; for the word which our Bible translates as "Saviour" means originally rescuer or deliverer, one bringing help when we ourselves are no longer able to help ourselves.

The Holy Scriptures do not leave in doubt what sort of need is meant here—from which only a Saviour, a deliverer, can rescue us. They speak plainly of sin and mean thereby our disobedience against God's holy commandments, the impudent mutiny of the human creature against his Creator. And the Scriptures trace this perversion in the basic human attitude toward God back to the first beginnings of the human race and regard pessimistically all human striving for improving this condition: "Every imagination of the thoughts of his heart was only evil continually" (Genesis 6: 5). Death and judgment are the end; for "the wages of sin is death" (Romans 6: 23), and God "shall reward every man according to his works" (Matthew 16: 27).

To recognize the truth of such a verdict we need not follow human history step by step; a glance at our own heart and life—when they are honourable—shows us more clearly than all examples that we cannot abide one instant before the holy God and His commandments, and that in reality all the misery of our lives is well deserved if, yes, if there is a God in heaven who demands of us obedience to His holy will. This bad conscience is consequently almost always the secret mainspring of all crass or refined atheism and godlessness. For who could ever have found a way to redeem himself from his bad conscience, and therefore from his sins, other than to deny God, or to forget Him, or at least try to forget Him, and to place himself in God's place as his own legislator and lord?

Yet no one can escape from the grasp of God! "Whither shall I go from thy spirit? or whither shall I flee from thy presence? If I ascend up into heaven, thou art there: if I make my bed in hell, behold thou art there. If I take the wings of the morning, and dwell in the uttermost parts of the sea; even there shall thy hand lead me, and thy right hand shall hold me" (Psalm 139: 7–10). There is no escaping from God and none may elude His judgment. It is therefore hardly astonishing that this earth is becoming more and more a hell, that a battle of all against all rages here; but it is astonishing when, to this human world, these tidings are proclaimed: "Unto you is born this day . . . a Saviour, which is Christ the Lord."

Of course *how* this promised salvation will occur, *how* our deliverance takes place, is not told us in the Christmas gospel; but it had already been foreshadowed and ushered in. The seer of Isaiah 53 had foreseen it: "Surely he hath borne our griefs, and carried our sorrows." A pious man has coined this fine saying, "The passion of Christ begins with his swaddling clothes." In Christ, God Himself brings the deliverance which we are unable to secure for ourselves: He not only inclines toward us, but lifts us toward Himself: "I will forgive their iniquity, and I will remember their sin no more" (Jeremiah 31: 34). Christ, the "God with us," is also the "God for us," and we may joyfully cry out, "If God be for us, who can be against us?" (Romans 8: 31).

That is truly a proclamation which deserves the name "great joy." Fear may now withdraw: "Fear not: for, behold, I bring you good tidings of great joy, which shall be to all people." Surely this is a joy which passeth all understanding; for it concerns God's work and activity, and how could we understand that? This joy is more than what we human beings may ever dare to expect and hope. But it is an object of petition, it is to be believed. And who believes has!

It is to the shepherds that was given the first information about the Saviour who lies as a babe in the manger. They are simple, plain, people: "to the poor" is the gospel preached (Luke 4: 18). They certainly did not have unlimited wishes and no grandiose hopes for their earthly existence; they assuredly did not dream of a Paradise on earth that was soon to come. And whoever does so will always disregard the Biblical tidings about Christ. But he who wishes to reach again an agreement with God and seeks peace of mind may and must be helped. The glad tidings of Christmas proclaim to him: "God is near, to help you; Jesus Christ, your brother and your Saviour, is here; fear not, only believe!"

And we, dear friends, who are cut off from the outside world, inactive spectators of all men's battles and convulsions, we who have daily many hours to gaze inwardly and to understand ourselves clearly, we who often miss so painfully the peace of mind because we do not look at God and His word, but rather at mortals and their doings —should not our inward hearing be especially receptive to the tidings brought to us by the Christmas gospel? Should not the saying about the "great joy" concern us in particular, since we know fear—fear of death as well as fear of life? Let us therefore today, on this holy Christmas Eve, beseech the Lord Jesus Christ that he, who came as a babe into a world alienated from God in order to save it, may enter also into us, bring us his salvation, and grant us his joy! Amen.

II

NEW YEAR'S EVE 1944

Lord, now lettest thou thy servant depart in peace, according to thy word: for mine eyes have seen thy salvation, which thou hast prepared before the face of all people; a light to lighten the Gentiles, and the glory of thy people Israel.

Luke 2: 29–32

THE OLD year inclines toward its end. In a few hours it will become a memory for us and then we shall enter into a new one, which, veiled in fog and gloom, waits for us. It is therefore natural that our thoughts should wander backwards, and that we attempt to balance the books, so to speak, in order that we may know what we may bring into the new life period that opens before us.

This much is certain for us all: the year now ending closes with a deficit! We have waited days, weeks, and months; all of us have mobilized our patience, in order to pass from one day to the next, again and again. But what has come from our waiting? We have hoped, we have repeatedly thought that at last the moment was near when our lot would improve, when the door of our prison must finally open; and we have altered the whole force of our beliefs, all our optimism, in order not to break down. But where have we arrived with all our hoping? We have often taken our heart in both hands and have comforted it: "Be still, my heart!" when it would cry out too painfully in its disquiet. However, it has been a miserable venture because, aside from our own affliction, the grief of the whole world weighed us down—a world crying for peace out of the depths of its torments. True, we have occasionally had some small gleams of light which made us happy for a few hours, but they were counter-balanced by painful experiences which were our lot and made our days twice as dark.

When all is said, a real favourable balance remained to none of us, as far as we can see. We are inclined to write off the whole year 1944 as a loss, and to make a wholly new beginning with the New Year in the slight hope that conditions may improve, so as not to bring us again such a complete disappointment of all our wishes and expectations. One of us may have a little more confidence in the future than another in our midst; but trust is hardly very strong any more in any of us: we have seen and endured too much, and our inner strength is not inexhaustible.

Thus we are rather perplexed at the end of this year, and often may be confronted by the question whether this life be worth living—worth the daily waiting, hoping, and struggling.

Now the Gospel places before us a man whose whole life was a single waiting, the aged Simeon. We know little about him: he appears only in this passage, and then he vanishes forever from our sight. And yet he is one of the most impressive Biblical characters, although we know neither his ancestry nor his profession, as also nothing else of his personal situation is known. What is told us about him is merely that he was "just and devout," and therefore belonged to the good, pious, humble classes, which were of course numerous. And we may infer from the circumstances that he must have been quite old. These particulars are not in the least calculated to make a person appear interesting or important.

There is, however, one detail about this man that rivets our attention, the sole matter which likewise seemed to the Evangelist worthy of notice in the life and deeds of

this old man: he was "waiting." And this waiting, even
if it continued, as seems probable, through years and decades,
was not in vain, but ended in a prayer of thanksgiving and
a hymn of praise. We gain the impression of seeing here
before us one of the few really happy persons who have
been or are still on this earth. For whoever is able to say,
"Lord, now lettest thou thy servant depart in peace,"
should obviously be called happy, because for him life
was fulfilled in its most essential hope, toward which
it aimed.

We know of course that this does not happen for all
waiting. A German proverb says, "Hoping and waiting
drive some mad" [or, "Hope deferred maketh the heart
sick" (Proverbs 13: 12)]. We ourselves know likewise
from personal, bitter experience that hope and realization
are at times widely separated and often never come together.
But the waiting of the old Simeon has its own, singularly
peculiar, character: he was "waiting for the consolation of
Israel," i.e., his hope was centred in what God had promised
His people as a comfort in its misery. In other words, his
hope was inspired by those prophetic voices which told
of the coming redemption, of God's Anointed who would
again set right the erring people—nay, not only the people
of Israel, for it is said of him that he would be "a light
to lighten the Gentiles" (Luke 2: 32). In this waiting,
Simeon relied on this word of God, and in addition he
received (according to the Gospel) a personal revelation of
the Holy Spirit announcing that "he should not see death,
before he had seen the Lord's Christ" (Luke 2: 26). He
then waited in this hope, year after year, in the assurance
that God Himself had said it. The fact that others about
him had long since given up this hope did not concern
him; that year after year rolled by did not perplex him;
that he himself was on the way to the grave, approaching
it with every step, could not extinguish the joy of his

B

expectation, but only increased the longing for the fulfillment promised him. And so he waited and hoped. And
to him it happened according to the saying of the Scriptures: "Hope maketh not ashamed" (Romans 5: 5).

May perhaps this waiting of the old Simeon be of help
to us in our distress? Certainly not in the sense that we
draw from it the conclusion: "Do not let hope vanish, and
all will be well in the end!" Perhaps one may say so
today; but, as a result, tomorrow one will be quicker in
reaching the conclusion that all hoping is in vain. Paul's
saying that hope makes us not ashamed does not express a
truth of universal validity, to be proved by anyone, in all
circumstances. And this applies to all Biblical sayings which
have apparently a general validity. When Jesus says, "Ask,
and it shall be given you; seek, and ye shall find; knock,
and it shall be opened unto you: for every one that asketh
receiveth; and he that seeketh findeth; and to him that
knocketh it shall be opened" (Matthew 7: 7-8)—well:
many a one asks without ever receiving, many a one seeks
and never finds, and many a one knocks but there is neither
voice nor answer!

But this waiting of Simeon's may of course tell us one
thing, and tell it with emphasis: "Whoever waits for what
God has promised him assuredly does not wait in vain.
He may hopefully look forward, with patience and joy,
to the day on which he will see before his eyes the goal
of his waiting." Thus we face the questions, What are
you waiting for? What is the goal of your hopes?

Do we wish liberty for ourselves in the New Year?
Well, that is easily understood. But we do not have any
promise whatsoever of God that this gift will be granted
us. We are told, however, that we shall "through much
tribulation enter into the kingdom of God" (Acts 14: 22).
In the year 1945 we hope for the return of peace, for our
nations and for ourselves: good and well, may God grant

it to us. But if He does not do it . . . He has not committed Himself by a single word. He has, however, announced to us through the Lord Christ that in the last days, before the beginning of His Kingdom, the world will echo with wars and rumours of war.

But if precisely what moves our hearts most is excluded from God's promise, then we do indeed ask whether it is really worth our while to depend entirely in our waiting on a single word of the divine promise, as did the old Simeon? If God cannot help us in this, our most crushing affliction, is it still sensible to expect and hope anything else from Him? So asks human defiance, which wishes to go its own way; so asks human despair, which trusts God no more than its own weakness. It would therefore be truly better for us to search God's word, as did the ancient pious and God-fearing believers, one of whom was that Simeon, for what He promises those who remain steadfast in obedience and patient expectation. We long for liberty; yet liberty per se need not be a piece of good luck. But in God's omnipotence it has been said to us, "If the Son therefore shall make you free, ye shall be free indeed" (John 8: 36). We long for peace, but we do not know whether the coming peace will be worse than all the tribulation of this war. Yet we may hear from the lips of Jesus this saying: "Peace I leave with you, my peace I give unto you: not as the world giveth, give I unto you" (John 14: 27). And this peace, as the Apostle says, "passeth all understanding" (Philippians 4: 7), meaning everything that human beings may conceive as peace. To wait for this should be well worth while in the end.

But Simeon stands before us not only as the waiting man, but, as we see here, likewise as a man whose expectation became fulfillment, whose hope became reality—and his hymn of praise testifies to it. He has probably considered the long waiting as a bondage; but from this bondage he is now freed. He has noticed that his life lacked peace, but he has now found this peace. The fetters have dropped off from him, and peace has now taken up its abode in him.

And what has brought about this change—we may well say this miracle—in the old man? He tells himself, "Mine eyes have seen thy salvation." What actually happened? Simeon came into the Temple through some inner compulsion. He saw there a man and a woman engaged in offering for their first-born the sacrifice prescribed by the Law. He took the infant in his arms and sang his hymn of praise. I am convinced that the people who saw this scene wondered at that peculiar old man, and those who knew him must have thought, "Here we see it again, 'Hoping and waiting drive some mad'; and now old Simeon has caught it too!"

But the old man has different eyes than these people: unto him the eyes have been opened, as they were opened to the shepherds through the message of the angels, and he knows that this babe is none other than the promised "Lord's Christ." Therefore his seer's gaze reaches over space and time, into the future and over the whole earth. It is not merely the end of his personal waiting and hoping that matters: here the yearning of the whole world is gratified. God's promise to the fathers is fulfilled, and now here is what the nations waited for: God's "salvation" (Luke 2: 30) or, as Luther translated, consciously departing from the original Greek, the "Saviour."

But is that really the fulfillment? Simeon takes it as such. He calls the child whom he holds in his arms, "a light to lighten the Gentiles" and "the glory of thy people Israel" (2: 32). He is convinced: in this child there is present the one who removes the darkness in which the nations no longer could see God and recognize His ways. In this child has come the one for whose sending Israel will praise God's fidelity.

Is he right in this? Darkness still rests over the nations. And even if we may have formerly contested this, because we believe in human progress, at the end of this year we can no longer believe in it. The people of Israel could do nothing better with this Saviour than to try him and hand him over to the executioners. "His own received him not" (John 1: 11). And yet the fulfillment is there! Simeon saw it and he did not remain the only one: John the Baptist saw it when over one that was baptized by him the heavens opened and a voice said, "This is my beloved son." The disciples recognized it when through the lips of Peter they made this profession of faith: "Thou art the Christ, the Son of the living God" (Matthew 16: 16); and so many, many others, from the adulterous woman at Jacob's well to the heathen centurion under the cross. Of course in every case there is something peculiar about this recognition: it does not occur like a natural phenomenon, which forces itself upon people whether they wish it or not, but it comes as a question which requires a personal answer from each individual. There lies the babe in the manger or in the arms of his mother; there a teacher speaks in parables of the Kingdom of God; there a man hangs from the cross in death agonies of body and soul; and every time God asks, "Will you accept him as my Saviour?" And the one answers, "Yes!"—and finds what he was seeking; and others cry out, "Away with him, away with him, crucify him" (John 19: 15)—and wait in vain through all eternity for another.

Simeon can express gratitude: "Mine eyes have seen thy salvation"; the disciple testifies, "We beheld his glory" (John 1: 14). They saw with the eyes of faith, which God had opened, while others saw nothing, even though their eyes looked at the same scene as a Simeon or a John. And so a judgment is fulfilled, separating faith from unbelief, as Jesus says: "For judgment I am come into this world,

that they which see not might see; and that they which
see might be made blind" (John 9: 39). But whoever
believes finds in this fulfillment the peace for which his soul
thirsts: "But as many as received him, to them gave he
power to become the sons of God" (John 1: 12). And Jesus
says of himself: "He that hath seen me hath seen the
Father" (John 14: 9). And where we see God as our
Father, there is freedom and peace.

This fulfillment which Simeon experienced and about
which the apostles bore witness is still ready for us at any
time, in the midst of our confinement and in the midst of
this war which shakes the world. It is not a fulfillment
which removes from us all anxieties and all privations; but
it is a fulfillment which takes away from every anxiety and
every privation the sting of bitterness, so that we fare like
Paul: "As unknown, and yet well known; as dying, and,
behold, we live; as chastened, and not killed; as sorrowful,
yet always rejoicing; as poor, yet making many rich; as
having nothing, and yet possessing all things" (2 Corinthians 6: 9–10).

What later became of the old man there in the Temple
we know not. It does not matter whether he lived to see
perhaps something of what was to come from this infant.
He lives in the assurance that God is faithful and so he is
ready to die as well as to live. He has seen God's salvation
and knows that God's promises, the fulfillment of which
is yet to come, will be likewise realized without fail.

So we also, my friends, may bid farewell to the old year
with a grateful retrospective glance. God has sent His
Saviour, and He has sent him for us too. And we may
cling to him in faith, no matter what troubles have come,
and may yet come, upon us. We are free in our faith in
him, for God has made us His children. And in the hope
for him we have peace, for no one can tear us away from
the grasp of his hand. Therefore we may begin with

renewed confidence the New Year, even though we do not know what it will bring us. We are waiting not only for the deliverance from this earthly captivity and not only for the end of this horrid war: we may look beyond all this to the greatest, to the conclusive deeds of God which have been promised to us, when God will establish His Kingdom in power, when we shall live before Him in the glorious freedom of the children of God, when there will be no end to peace, when the Lord Christ will return in order to make all who have believed in him in the shape of a servant fellow heirs of his glory.

> He has said it, and so my heart
> Chances it, glad and resolute,
> And feels no more dread's horror.
> > Amen.

III

SEPTUAGESIMA SUNDAY
JANUARY 28, 1945

For the kingdom of heaven is like unto a man that is an householder, which went out early in the morning to hire labourers into his vineyard. And when he had agreed with the labourers for a penny a day, he sent them into his vineyard. And he went out about the third hour, and saw others standing idle in the marketplace, and said unto them: Go ye also into the vineyard, and whatsoever is right I will give you. And they went their way. Again he went out about the sixth and ninth hour, and did likewise. And about the eleventh hour he went out, and found others standing idle, and saith unto them, Why stand ye here all the day idle? They say unto him, Because no man has hired us. He saith unto them, Go ye also into the vineyard, and whatsoever is right, that shall ye receive. So when even was come, the lord of the vineyard saith unto his steward, Call the labourers, and give them their hire, beginning from the last unto the first. And when they came that were hired about the eleventh hour, they received every man a penny. But when the first came, they supposed that they should have received more; and they likewise received every man a penny. And when they had received it, they murmured against the goodman of the house, saying, These last have wrought but one hour, and thou hast made them equal unto us, which have borne the burden and heat of the day. But he answered one of them, and said, Friend, I do thee no wrong: didst thou not agree with me for a penny? Take that thine is, and go thy way: I will give unto this last, even as unto thee. Is it not lawful for me to do what I will with mine own? Is thine eye evil, because I am good? So the last shall be first, and the first last.

Matthew 20: 1-16

WHEN ON New Year's Eve, in our last service, the picture of the waiting Simeon appeared before our eyes we all

24

felt that we were addressed directly, for we also are waiting persons and precisely in our captivity we are ever again waiting persons. On the contrary, this immediate contact is lacking in today's Gospel lesson: it does not appear—at least at first glance—to bring a message pertinent to our present state, for it deals with hiring, with work and its compensation, in other words, with matters alien to us in our forced idleness. The twelve apostles, to whom according to the Evangelist's account Jesus told this parable, had already been called to do his work, they had already had their first experiences as his messengers and would soon —after Good Friday, Easter, and Pentecost—initiate their great world mission.

But we do not know whether the Lord Christ still has a task for us, whether he has assigned us yet a time of free activity, or whether also for us the eleventh hour has already passed. In this respect this Gospel lesson sounds different for our ears than for those of the Christian congregation gathered in the churches at home, which faces so many urgent tasks and labours, different also from what it may have sounded formerly to ourselves, when, still in the midst of this great Christian congregation, we were called to action and work.

Nevertheless, it is the peculiarity of the word of God that it demands to be heard by us in any situation and at any time, because in any situation and at any time it has the message we need.

The first thing that is told us in this parable is this: when the Kingdom of Heaven comes, the hiring of labourers is prominent. The householder goes out in the morning to hire labourers for his vineyard. When therefore the Lord Jesus Christ announces, "The Kingdom of Heaven is at hand," he does not announce thereby an event which matures and reaches completion, like a change in the weather or a natural catastrophe; then inevitably it affects everyone within its sphere of influence no matter whether he wishes it or not. On the contrary, everyone to whom that message comes is invited to take a personal attitude and decision: "The Kingdom of Heaven is at hand, therefore do penance, therefore change your disposition!" And then he is hired for work, as it says here in this parable, "Go ye into the vineyard."

We are thus clearly told that our faith never can and never should be a mere rest pillow, as the words of Jesus often stress elsewhere: "Not every one that saith unto me, Lord, Lord, shall enter into the kingdom of heaven; but he that doeth the will of my Father which is in heaven" (Matthew 7: 21). Or, "Whosoever heareth these sayings of mine, and doeth them, I will liken him unto a wise man, which built his house upon a rock" (Matthew 7: 24). Therefore, the type of Christianity which isolates itself, which allows the wicked world to follow its course, and is content to hope for a better hereafter, is nothing but a caricature, a foolish cartoon. The terrestrial life of Jesus himself, as also the activity of his apostles, proves it by showing how the Gospel is a power of God which constantly urges forward to action, to work while it is still day. And wherever there has been real, living faith in Christ, there work has been accomplished, beginning with the apostles in the time of the Book of Acts, beginning with a Paul, who could say of himself, "I laboured more abundantly than they all" (1 Corinthians 15: 10), down to a Pastor Bodelschwingh, who spurred his missionaries to greater zeal and warned them saying, "Please, not so slow; otherwise they die in the meantime"—meaning the Negroes in East Africa to whom he sent them.

Here, of course, is a difficulty for us. By "vineyard" we understand with good reason God's congregation on this earth, both the existing one and the one newly formed here and there through the preaching of the gospel. In this sense the figure of the vineyard is already used in the Old Testament, and in his parable Jesus undoubtedly meant it so. In this "vineyard of the Lord" there is always much work: there are thousands to be comforted, invalids to be nursed, doubters to be strengthened, strayers to be rightly guided. Only for us there is nothing to do there because, without our participation and without our will, we with our Christian faith are forcibly isolated; because the lot God has assigned us is named "solitude." Is there anything at all that we can do? Does the Lord Christ hire us for work, even here, or must we say with those unemployed of the eleventh hour, "No man hath hired us"? It would be ominous for us to become fixed in this conviction, and so deny all personal blame and attribute to God, who has brought us to this state, all the responsibility.

In reality we are indeed called by God to His service, and none of us is excepted. All of us are told, "Go ye also into the vineyard!" We are not so alone in our isolation that we no longer have a Christian brother at our side to whom, as to our neighbour, we are referred through God's commandment, in order to further, rather than hinder, his faith. And even if we were in strictest solitary confinement, God's call to us would remain in force.

The Apostle Paul writes in the first letter to his Corinthians, "Ye are God's husbandry, ye are God's building" (3: 9). "Ye"—that is the totality, but it is also every individual in this totality, as we read in the same letter, in another passage: "Know ye not that your body is the temple of the Holy Ghost which is in you, which ye have of God, and ye are not your own?" (6: 19). We do not belong to ourselves: God, in the holy baptism, has laid claim on us as His property. There is therefore work in God's service for us, if only we have ears to hear His call; there is a divine service in our own behalf, if we are ready to do for Him this service on behalf of His property. And the means placed in our hand for such work in God's service are called God's word and prayer.

Dear friends, we have so many silent hours in our life here. But just because they are silent hours they need not be empty hours. It certainly is not God's intention for us that we should become poorer in the eternal treasure while in the solitude which He has imposed upon us; nor that these months and years should pass away without any fruit growing therefrom. True: He wishes to be entreated, and always anew and always more faithfully does He wish to be entreated. And this is the most rewarding work to which He now calls us.

In the Epistle of James there is this saying: "Pure religion and undefiled before God and the Father is this, To visit the fatherless and widows in their affliction, and to keep himself unspotted from the world" (James 1: 27). From the first part of this service—namely, service to the neighbours who need us—we are to a great extent precluded; but the second part—namely, keeping ourselves unspotted from the world—demands that we turn hand and heart to it, that we open to God the access to His temple, that we cultivate the field of our heart for Him in order that His seed may take root, grow, and mature. And if it is now perhaps the eleventh hour, if before the end only a few weeks remain for us to spend here in silence, yet there is time for us to hear the call and go to do the work Christ has ordained for us.

And this service which God requires of us pays! This is the second matter of which our Gospel lesson speaks with all clearness. The householder came to an agreement with the workers about wages of a penny a day. And even to those who were in his employ one brief last hour of the day he promised, "Whatsoever is right I will give you."

There was a time, and it was not so long ago, when the thought of a reward was banned and proscribed in every moral and religious consideration. Idealism, so called, set up the lofty goal of doing the good for its own sake, and asserted that even the thought of rewards robbed every good action of its genuine goodness. But through this idea people have not become better or less selfish. The Bible does not reckon with an ideal picture, nor with a human being who seeks the good for its own sake and rejects the evil on its own account; for such a human being does not exist, has never existed, will never exist. The Bible addresses the real human being, who figures, for his own benefit, the results of his conduct and plans his activity so that it will bring him closer to his goal or goals. We as prisoners know quite well that it is simply impossible to devote oneself for a considerable length of time to an activity which seems purposeless and aimless, in short, to deeds which in our opinion do not pay. Accordingly, God's work speaks repeatedly and most candidly of rewards. And this is not, perchance, a lapse from good taste due to the Old Testament, which has been essentially removed and eliminated by the message of Jesus! Jesus speaks again and again, with utter candour, of the reward of human activity, at times in parables, as in today's Gospel lesson or in the Parable of the Talents, but also literally, as in the Sermon on the Mount or in the speech on the Last Judgment. God does not allow Himself to be served without compensation like a master of slaves or a tyrant, but He gives, for every honest work performed in His service, the exactly appropriate remuneration.

What this remuneration consists of is not specified exactly in our parable. Only one matter is stressed—each labourer was paid one penny, without consideration of the amount of work he accomplished: the Lord makes no differences in His compensation. This presents some difficulties for us, inasmuch as in the Parable of the Talents one servant is set over ten cities, the other, according to his lesser accomplishment, over five, while the lazy servant was deprived of the single talent entrusted to him, which was then added to the ten of the first servant. Here, on the contrary, everyone receives the same amount as his wages, the one penny agreed upon as a day's pay. Jesus cannot have meant to say anything but that God gives the full compensation to everyone who is employed by Him and continues in His service until the end of the working day, whether he toiled a long or a short time after he was set to work.

And this compensation, according to all that the New Testament says, consists in being allowed to have God as our Father—all of us who follow the call of Jesus—from the first of the twelve apostles to be called to the thief on the cross, who still heard the call at the end of the eleventh hour. This compensation consists in the full participation in the redeeming work of Jesus Christ on the part of all who obey—early or late—his call to follow him and thereby be employed by him. A wretched publican and sinner, such as Matthew-Levi, was employed not otherwise than a zealous and pious observer of the Law, such as Paul was before he experienced his Damascus road.

Here, however, the purport of the figurative sense of the parable breaks down. On the one hand, we have God's fatherly forgiving love, freely given to us, and the atoning death of Jesus on the cross for our sake; on the other, "a penny," the mere daily wages for our paltry work. An earthly employer could not pay wages in this manner even figuratively. The word "wages" acquires here an entirely different and new sense. We understand as wages something of value corresponding to the exertion put forth. But this is no longer in question: God gives lavishly above all that we may request or understand, let alone deserve. He deals with us not like an employer, according to performance and corresponding compensation, but like a father, who gives his whole heart, replete with fatherly, divine love and mercy, to his prodigal son, returning from his wretched ruin, no less than to his obedient son, without losing anything thereby out of the abundance of his wealth. He is and remains rich far above all those who cry unto Him.

May we say, "No man hath hired us," because we are imprisoned behind barbed wire and iron bars, and relegated to solitude? No, my friends, God invites us to reach out in prayer for this love of His, for this compensation of His, for thus it has been promised: "Whosoever shall call on the name of the Lord shall be saved" (Acts 2: 21). And the Lord Christ has confirmed it: "Blessed are they which do hunger and thirst after righteousness: for they shall be filled" (Matthew 5: 6). God compensates for the work to which He calls us; and He compensates for it beyond all understanding: happy are we with such an excellent Lord!

Now, it happens that in the Parable of the Labourers in the Vineyard the first comers to the work murmured because the others who came later, including even those who had toiled merely a single hour, received the same wages as they themselves did. And these people, according to our normal human feeling, are absolutely right—no question about it. If a human employer acted in this manner he would not only be a poor businessman, but through such conduct he would also undermine all labour principles and all the foundations for a social justice. But what we have here is not a story about human communal life, but merely a parable of the Kingdom of God; not an earthly employer, but the Father in heaven; not a compensation corresponding to our performance, but God's lavish gift to His children; not money or money values, but God's love—His mercy and loving-kindness—which saves sinful men from perdition and transfers them into the Kingdom of Heaven.

There are of course people who have been called by God in the early morning of their lifetime and have then entered His employment. And there are others who are reached by His call only later. And finally there are also those who perceive the calling voice more or less at the last minute. To be sure, these are differences—nay, humanly speaking really notable differences. But even in the case of those who came first, it is certain that they did not deserve the great gift of God as an earned, rightfully theirs, compensation—love in general can never be earned. True, a father may say to his erring son, "All right, I shall forgive you; but you must earn my love afresh." But in reality he merely wishes to see a proof that the son is really eager for his father's love, and when he sees this proof he again bestows his affections on the youth: he gives them freely anew. We may earn monetary compensation, praise, recognition, but love is always given freely, and this applies incomparably to God's love. When therefore pious persons, called from their youth, look contemptuously upon others who have spent the greatest part of their life far from God but at last listen to His call—perhaps at the eleventh hour —and can then devote to Him nothing but the pitiful remains of their life's strength and time; when these pious souls then begin to murmur, deploring that such people should be considered their equals, as children of God and as receiving His promises; when they feel that they themselves had really earned something better—they, the faithful and steadfast—in comparison with these who have been saved from perdition with considerable toil and trouble—then comes to pass that about which Jesus wished to warn his disciples: then the first shall be last and, in their place, the last first.

God's love is what He gives us; it is His loving-kindness that has made us His children. And so, as His children, we are the "first," so intimately close to His paternal heart that no one and nothing may separate us from Him—even if we separate ourselves from Him. As long as we accept His love for what it is—namely, an inconceivably grand gift which through faith gives to our life a firm foundation, through love guides our activity in the right direction, and through hope removes the sting from our death—during all this time we remain in the communion with our heavenly Father, so that we can but love God in return and our neighbour as ourselves.

But when it comes to pass that we no longer are able to look at our neighbour with the eyes of love, no longer as the one who is loved by God no less than we are—loved so that God has given for His sake also His only begotten son—then we no longer abide in God's love, as His children, and as the first, close to His heart. Nay, we have even reached criticism of God and we place our own concept of justice against the bottomless and shoreless love of God, which is the sole source of our life.

So now we must start again from the beginning. We were "the first," but we have become "the last" because we are no longer children of God, but merely mortals who presume to strive with God and who, instead of serving God in love and gratitude, would make their own purposes available to God. This, however, remains always a futile exertion, for God always has ready the reply of His omnipotence: "Is it not lawful [or, "Do I not have the power"] to do what I will with mine own?" (Matthew

c

20: 15). These words also are added: "Take that thine is, and go thy way" (20: 14). So we have a penny in our hand, and absolutely nothing more. The sun goes down in our life, because we must recognize that the wages we have earned are really nothing and God's love was everything—the love of God to which we, with our principles of justice—behind which our uncharitable selfishness was hidden—intended to teach a lesson.

My friends, all this is unfortunately no mere pale theory. Otherwise the Lord Jesus would not have needed to give this warning to his disciples, and the apostles would not have felt the urge to preserve it and write it down. The old Adam in us keeps on making comparisons and lifts himself above his fellow servant, believing himself to be superior to him. We must therefore discipline him earnestly and thoroughly. For wherever he gets the upper hand, the service of God is really at an end. Then the saying, "Take that thine is, and go thy way," becomes positively a dismissal, and all that we intend to do later in God's service loses entirely its significance and value. "Many will say to me in that day, Lord, Lord, have we not prophesied in thy name? and in thy name have cast out devils? and in thy name done many wonderful works? And then will I profess unto them, I never knew you: depart from me, ye that work iniquity" (Matthew 7: 22–23). And when the Lord Jesus has thus made clear for us that God's service cannot go hand in hand with an unloving attitude toward our neighbour, there remains but one thing for us. It is not that we should force ourselves to feel brotherly love, for just as love cannot be earned so love cannot be forced. But this is the way to fight the old Adam in ourselves: to pray God that He might make His love very great for us, so that it will fill our heart. Then our love for our neighbour acquires new strength and we recognize in our fellow servant a brother with whom we should praise in unison the mercy and the goodness of our Father in heaven; nay, we may then praise Him in the community of God's redeemed children. And so shall we do! Yes, "Thanks be unto God for his unspeakable gift" (2 Corinthians 9: 15). Amen.

IV

REMINISCERE SUNDAY
FEBRUARY 25, 1945

Then Jesus went thence, and departed into the coasts of Tyre
and Sidon. And, behold, a woman of Canaan came out of the
same coasts, and cried unto him, saying, Have mercy on me, O
Lord, thou Son of David; my daughter is grievously vexed with a
devil. But he answered her not a word. And his disciples came
and besought him, saying, Send her away; for she crieth after us.
But he answered and said, I am not sent but unto the lost sheep
of the house of Israel. Then came she and worshipped him, saying,
Lord, help me. But he answered and said, It is not meet to take
the children's bread, and to cast it to dogs. And she said, Truth,
Lord: yet the dogs eat of the crumbs which fall from their masters'
table. Then Jesus answered and said unto her, O woman, great is
thy faith: be it unto thee even as thou wilt. And her daughter was
made whole from that very hour.

Matthew 15: 21-28

THIS IS one of the so-called miracle stories of the Bible, one
of those narratives dating from the earliest times of the
Christian faith about which discussion has raged for a
century—dismissing them finally as pious legends. For
some time now such disputes have ceased to be mentioned.
First of all because, owing to the great lapse of time and
the insufficiency of data, a final conclusion, which would
really be historical and scholarly, is no longer possible;
but in the second place—and this is the vital point—because
it has been noticed that in most of these so-called miracle
stories the emphasis is not on the miracle per se, but on
the circumstances that induced the Lord Christ to do
something at which his hearers and disciples marvelled, or
should have marvelled.

36

In today's Gospel lesson it is wholly manifest that the healing of the ailing girl is only incidental in the whole narrative; moreover, it is utterly insignificant in this instance whether we think we can explain this healing or regard it as something inexplicable, namely, a miracle. The central, stressed feature, in reality, is the battle of wits between the mother and the Lord, and precisely there lies the bearing of this story, which concerns us directly even now. Yes, precisely in this battle a real miracle takes place, something at which we must marvel no less than the Lord Jesus did at the time. He was so astonished, as we are told, that he finally granted her request and said to her, "O woman, great is thy faith." And in this word of Jesus we have at the same time the key to the understanding of the whole incident. We have here before us an instance of "great faith"—a faith such as Jesus met extremely seldom in his life on earth.

In the New Testament we read repeatedly of the obstinate unbelief of the contemporaries of Jesus, and particularly of his closer Nazareth townsmen. We hear him lament over the little faith of his disciples and followers. A "great faith" which evoked a word of glad astonishment he found only in the centurion of Capernaum, who beseeched him for the healing of his ailing servant, and in this Syrian mother driven to him by her anxiety over her daughter. Jesus noticed the greatness of the centurion's faith because he disclosed an absolute trust in the almighty power of Jesus: "Speak the word only, and my servant shall be healed" (Matthew 8: 8). In the case of this woman something different, something greater, is involved: we may perhaps say, the constancy of faith; but even more, as we shall see.

Exactly like the centurion, this woman does not belong to the people of Israel: she is a "heathen," as we should

say, and as such she has no immediate claim to the help
of the Jewish Messiah. Nothing at all indicates that she was
a proselyte, participating in the worship of Israel, as was
the case with the centurion of Capernaum. And so she
has nothing to which she might appeal and through which
she might add force to her plea. For Jesus she is neither a
fellow citizen nor a fellow believer, but from every point
of view an alien. What nevertheless sends her to him is
solely her great distress, the affliction of her daughter
which the mother feels and bears wholly as her own
burden and which brings from her lips the urgent cry,
"Lord, help me." Behind these words is the slight hope
that the man she is pursuing with her cries can and will
help her. She addresses him as "O Lord, thou Son of
David." Somehow she has heard that in this Jesus, according to the rumour that preceded him, had appeared the
Saviour, whose coming had been awaited for many genera-
tions by the neighbouring Jewish people. This is enough
for her, and now she simply has recourse to him in her
need. She did the right thing.

Even at the beginning the woman stands before us as
a believer, and even this faith goes beyond ordinary,
everyday standards. We human beings are always inclined
to think that on our part we need to supply certain conditions in order to have faith. We have the feeling—rooted
in the depths of our being—that in order to appear before
God we may not come with empty hands, that we must
have something to present to Him, be it a regular material
offering, as in the most primitive religions, be it a certain
minimum of religious convictions to which we may appeal,
be it a certain moral excellence which shall make us agreeable and acceptable in the sight of God.

But with reference to the Lord Christ all this is nothing
but a superstition, which far from helping us may hinder
us from really going to him, and be truly earnest in our

faith in him and in his help. With regard to him, we are told, "You may and you must come just as you are!" His glad tidings, and consequently his beatitudes, are addressed to the poor and suffering, who have nothing and can give nothing, the hungry and thirsty. He invites the troubled and heavy laden to come unto him; nay, it is to the sinners that he wishes to give his help. We must therefore guard against yielding to that excessively human feeling which would persuade us thus: Since I am spiritually as poor and empty as a beggar, who has nothing to give, I cannot turn unto God; since I am not sufficiently pious, believing, self-collected, I cannot pray to Him.

From my own experience of these years, I know how, precisely in our situation with its monotonous uniformity, with its enormous distress that weighs upon us like an unalterable destiny, with its apparent hopelessness, such thoughts come and oppress us, and how they gnaw the root of our faith. It is therefore essential that we recollect —I would like to say, daily anew—what we have heard about this Jesus and that we then go to him with our burden, and in "comforted despair," as Martin Luther named it, cry unto him, "Lord, help me"—as this poor heathen woman did. For this is faith—not some kind of orthodoxy, not some moral excellence, absolutely nothing that we bring along; nay, this is faith, that I bring to the Lord Jesus Christ my distress, in the assurance, or even only in the slight hope, that God has sent him for me, yes, for me indeed.

The faith of the woman is of course subjected to a hard test. Jesus does not even seem to hear her cries: "He answered her not a word." The situation arising from the cries of the woman and the silence of Jesus became so painful that the followers of Jesus intervened: "Send her away; for she crieth after us." It is not wholly certain whether these words mean only, "Send her away; tell her that you are not here for her!" or whether the words request that Jesus help her in order to be thus rid of her in an agreeable manner. But this is not of further significance, for even if compassion for the distressed woman was expressed by the disciples, it remains only—as not a little human compassion—a compassion which seeks first of all one's own ease; and their intercession, if it was such, remained entirely futile because Jesus did not allow motives of convenience to influence his action or inaction. He obeyed only to his commission, to the instructions his heavenly Father had given him; and this commission sent him only to "the lost sheep of the house of Israel." So he rejected sharply and unequivocally the interference of the people around him, and went on without paying the slightest attention to the woman.

What was taking place at that moment in the heart of the unfortunate woman we can only guess. She had received no answer to her appeal for help, and from the words of Jesus to the disciples she could infer that her hope and faith had been fruitless. No, for her and for her need this son of David was not available; and if she still had a spark of pride and self-respect she must desist from her purpose and disappear from the spot. This, in any case, would be the most natural reaction: a deliberately snubbed appeal for help arouses defiance in us, notably if, as here, the person entreated gives us explicitly to understand that he does not wish to listen.

Possibly we ourselves know something of such a crisis of faith. Possibly we also have once cried unto God really *de profundis*, out of the depths, because we simply did not know which way to turn—and God was silent. And then we stopped our cries and resigned ourselves to the inevitable, having the feeling that our faith had received a hard blow, from which it could recover only slowly and never entirely. To many a person, in such a trial of his faith, it has happened that his confidence that God was available also to him was lost forever. Nay, how many people around us may have called and cried unto God, precisely in these inexpressibly distressing days, because they see that here all hope in human help is vain—"But he answered . . . not a word." And how soon may not we ourselves find ourselves in the same state?

The woman in the Gospel withstood and overcame that blow. She could and would not admit that Jesus was not expressly available to her. He was her last, her sole hope, and she did not give up. So she came running and threw herself at the feet of Jesus, and now her appeal became nothing but a single cry: "Lord, help me." Pride and defiance were no longer in question, they had been discarded; but at least one result was achieved: now Jesus must speak to her directly, eye to eye, now the decision must be taken in all candour and clarity: a yes or a no. And again it is a "No!"—as a matter of fact an outspokenly harsh "No!" "It is not meet to take the children's bread, and cast it to dogs." The saying is extremely transparent: the children are the people of Israel, the dogs are the heathen. If this story were not so familiar to us, we should be horrified at the cutting sharpness, the mordant bitterness of this answer, with which Jesus rejected the desperate appeal of a poor mother for the rescue of her daughter. This does not belong to the traditional picture of Jesus as we know it; several other sayings of the Lord in the New Testament, likewise, are out of harmony with it. Jesus is decidedly not the soft and always courteous gentleman, who sees everything in the best light and is therefore inclined to be easy-going; far from that, he is always and with full awareness the envoy and the agent of God. Moreover, his God is not the good-natured universal Father, who with an understanding and forgiving smile sees from afar the hustle and bustle of men. No, He is

the merciful—and holy—God of the Bible, the Creator
of the whole world who even now, however, does not
allow the control to be taken from His hands; the Father
of all human beings who, however, does not in the least
refrain from summoning, as judge, His creatures to account.
From this God did Jesus receive his commission, and this
commission sent him to the people of Israel and not to
the heathen nations, as he had just told his disciples. This
limitation ended only with the death of Jesus; it was the
risen Lord who for the first time sent his apostles into the
wide world.

Thus, humanly speaking, the situation of the beseeching
woman has now really become utterly hopeless. The
answer she has received declares unmistakably that Jesus
cannot help her because he may not help her: "You have
no claim on me. The bread which I have to give belongs
to the children, and for that very reason I cannot cast it
to dogs."

And so it is really a miracle that the story does not end
here, that the faith of the woman still remains able to
sustain this strain. For, surely, the woman could still
protest against this decision, she could begin to dispute
and quarrel with the Lord Christ. We could understand
this well, and one could almost be inclined to give her the
text of the answer she should give: "On the contrary, we
heathen are also human beings, and perhaps better ones
than the Jews." With such a reply the story would be
actually ended, for then a human claim would be raised
against the commission of God, a chasm would be opened
over which not even the hand of Jesus could reach, because
he could do nothing against God's will and commission.
What about the other possibility, namely, that the
woman should accept the decision of Jesus and withdraw

as being definitely dismissed? Then also the interview
would come to its inconclusive end. It would be the
woman herself, then, who would draw back in fright
from the opened chasm without daring to leap over it.
Rebellion or resignation: in effect both come to the same
result. The bridge between God and me falls down if I
rebel, if I attempt to pass judgment on God's activity or
inactivity, and thus make myself His judge. And this
bridge remains untrodden, hence useless, if I become
resigned, if I infer from God's silence or speech a final
"No," and so reconcile myself and withdraw from Him.

The Canaanite woman does neither the one nor the
other. She answers, "Truth, Lord: yet the dogs eat of the
crumbs which fall from their masters' table." One could
think that this woman is shrewd and in fighting trim.
That may be, but it does not touch the core of the matter
in hand. This becomes clearer when we listen to the
literal translation of the answer: "Yes, Lord, for the puppies
eat only the crumbs which fall from the table of their
masters." She means to say: "You are perfectly right, one
should not cast the bread of the children to the dogs,
and I do not at all ask this of you. But when the children
are satiated, there fall crumbs from which the puppy under
the table may sustain his life."

This saying, and the whole attitude which is expressed
thereby, is what Jesus designates as the "great faith." In
this saying there is no rebellion against the humanly incomprehensible ordinance of God, which has granted the
Jews an advantage over their neighbours. This "Yes, Lord"
recognizes the sovereignty of God without any ifs and buts.
"He is the Lord, let Him do what pleases Him." "Who
am I that I should contest with God?" This is the exact
opposite of every rebellion, this is the humility of the

creature in the presence of his Creator—that humility without which no faith is possible, since a real faith can come to life only where I expect nothing from myself but, on the contrary, everything from God. Here indeed stands before us a person who really expects everything from God. Even behind the "No," which is suggested by the table of the children and which strikes the woman's ear harshly and distinctly, she perceives, nevertheless, with the delicate hearing of the soul the secret "Yes" which does not exclude her from the small space under the table with the little dogs. And this is the exact opposite of all resignation: it is that victorious faith for which the word "surrender" does not exist, for it knows that God is so excessively rich in grace and mercy that He has room for me and my misery. That is why Jesus calls the woman's faith "great": because she believes that God's grace is so great that no apparent dismissal, no matter how harsh, can separate her from the conviction: "In spite of everything, you are available for my need."

When I received from my lamented father the religious instruction leading to the confirmation, he closed his remarks on this passage with the words, "This woman is a veritable princess of Anhalt."[1] And with this the story really ends, for what follows, the explicit "Yes" that Jesus proclaims to the beseeching mother, the actual deliverance that brought recovery to her daughter, all this is only

[1][This expression is based on a German pun which cannot be reproduced in English. *Anhalt* is a former principality in the northern part of central Germany; its capital is Dessau. At the same time, the German *anhalten*, in the form *an sich halten*, has the meaning "to hold on to something, not to part with it." Thus one may say jocularly, "*Er ist aus Anhalt*" (he is from Anhalt) meaning, "he holds on to his money, he does not let it out of his hands." Thus Niemöller's father in applying to the Canaanitic woman the title of "princess of Anhalt" meant that she tenaciously clung to Jesus until he had granted her request. NOTE OF THE TRANSLATOR.]

the divine "Amen" to the answered prayer of this woman, which of course may not be omitted. The battle is ended, the trial has been withstood, and there remains for us the warning: "Fight—you also—the good fight of faith!"

True, there are not many people whose faith is subjected to so severe a test—no matter how dark the paths on which God leads some of us. But it may happen to us also, and it does occasionally happen, that from the portion meted out to us in our life we may gain the impression that God deliberately ignores us. I may think that He burdens me beyond my power to bear; my strength fails when I need it most; He leaves me in the lurch when I try to live my life in accordance with His commandments, as I would like to do; and so in all my difficulties I hear nothing but one "No" after the other. But this "No" should only make us realize that rightfully we can make no claim whatever on God; He invites us to be humble, to refrain from any attempt to gain His favour through some performance or other, and to pretend to really amount to something in God's presence.

But whoever endures this "No" in all submissiveness and relies on the undeserved free grace of God, which is so superabundant that even one like me does not appeal to Him in vain, he hears the stealthy "Yes" of God that brings the trial to an end. And this "Yes" is more easily perceptible for us than for the woman of today's Gospel lesson. For what did she actually know of Jesus of Nazareth, to whom she turned with her cry of distress? That he was considered the Messiah of the Jews and had helped not a few of his fellow citizens in their trouble—nothing more. We know him as the "man of sorrows," which he took upon himself for our sake, as the crucified and risen one, through whose death God spoke His ultimate "No" to all human attempts at self-aid, but at the same time the secret

"Yes" for all those who vindicate His judgment on us and, out of the fullness of His grace, accept as a gift what we need but lack.

As we look at the outcome of today's Gospel narrative we see clearly the way Jesus, as the good pastor, traversed with the poor woman in order to awaken in her the "great faith"; and it always happens likewise that we human beings recognize and understand from the end, looking back, the ways God travels with us. In your life and in my life it does not happen otherwise than with the Old Testament man of God to whom God said, "Thou canst not see my face . . . And I will take away mine hand, and thou shalt see my back parts" (Exodus 33: 20, 23). That may be sufficient for us. It will be sufficient for us if in our trials we remain convinced, like that woman, that God's grace is still abundant enough to embrace us; if we, like that woman, tirelessly persist in praying, and if necessary in pleading, to the one He has given us as Saviour: "Lord, help me!" For here the saying is indeed valid: "For every one that asketh receiveth; and he that seeketh findeth; and to him that knocketh it shall be opened." Amen.

V

MAUNDY THURSDAY
MARCH 29, 1945

For as often as ye eat this bread, and drink this cup, ye do shew
the Lord's death till he come.

1 Corinthians 11: 26

ON THE eve of that Good Friday on which three crosses
were erected on Golgotha, our Lord and Saviour gathered
about himself his more intimate circle of disciples—the
later apostles—for the last Paschal meal, for that remembrance meal through which God's people of the old covenant
recalled the wonderful rescue from the Egyptian bondage.
In accordance with the customary celebration of the
festival, they ate the Paschal lamb, drank the cup of thanksgiving, and sang together the great hymn of praise. Now
the celebration is finished and the disciples await the
evening departure to the usual lodging house outside the
city, on the Mount of Olives. But Jesus makes no move
to get ready to leave, but rather joins to the just-finished
Paschal meal a second solemn act. He takes the bread,
which is still lying on the table at which they had eaten,
breaks it in pieces, and gives it to the disciples with the
words: "Take, eat: this is my body, which is broken for
you: this do in remembrance of me" (1 Corinthians 11: 24).
Thereafter he took the cup, which was still standing before
him after the Paschal meal, passed it to his friends, and
said, "This cup is the new testament in my blood: this
do ye, as oft as ye drink it, in remembrance of me"
(1 Corinthians 11: 25).

47

At first, in their astonishment, the Twelve presumably did not know what was happening. But one thing they could not fail to hear, even in their first amazement: the Lord spoke here to them about his death. His body is broken like the bread that he distributes to them; his blood is shed like the draught of wine that he had given them to drink. His earthly life's work, hardly begun according to human reckoning, is finished: their Master takes leave from them.

According to what the Evangelists have recorded for us, this was not the first time Jesus spoke to his disciples about his impending death; but we always read, in connection with the preceding announcements of the coming sufferings, that they did not understand him. Jesus spoke to them in riddles when he said that his death was a divine necessity. They hoped for the inauguration of the Kingdom of God announced by him, they waited for the time when their Master would appear before the world as ruler and judge in order to usher in a new Golden Age. But now such a misunderstanding is no longer possible: all these dreams are at an end. One of the Twelve goes forth to betray his Lord, the others will be scattered, and the most loyal of them will deny that he had anything to do with this man. The whole thing is a catastrophe, an utter collapse!

Since that evening almost two thousand years have passed, and still now, and always, the disciples of Jesus gather again on the evening of Maundy Thursday around his table to partake of the meal to which the Lord invites them. Thereby they think of that hour in which Jesus ordered the disciples to observe this holy command. "This do in remembrance of me." Here one asks naturally— and who among us has never raised this question?—

"Fundamentally what is it that gives to this celebration its unparalleled power over the human heart? How does it happen that in spite of all theological disputations and schisms, which have flared up again and again, particularly about this sacrament, the Christian community continues to break the bread and partake of the cup as if all this strife did not concern it at all?"

Yes, my friends, it really does not concern the Christians at all. The Lord Jesus has given us no doctrines about this Holy Supper of his, nor did he wish to give us any such doctrines at all. All doctrines by which we try to assert something about God's activity are subject to the law of ageing and changing. What interested mightily the ancient Greeks, in their pious curiosity, namely, the question of how a man could be at the same time Son of God, involved theological disputations for centuries. They fought about it back and forth with arguments and counter-arguments. Today this no longer interests us in the least; not because we have become so much more indifferent about religion, but because we know that this is not a question which is connected with and rooted in the spirit of the New Testament and therefore in our Christian faith. Later periods have racked their brains trying to find out how it is possible that God, for the sake of Jesus, forgives the sins of those who believe in Him. How can He, if He is the holy and just God, place our sins upon another? Nowadays only some very learned theologians are accurately informed about these theories and mental exercises, while the Christian community has long since understood that a miracle cannot be explained, and consequently it is better to abstain from the attempt.

And in regard to the disputed questions about the Holy Supper the situation is not radically different. How can bread and wine be the body and blood of Jesus Christ?

D

The great division in the Reformation Church springs in a considerable measure from the different answers to this question. Luther taught differently from Zwingli in the matter, and the latter differently from Calvin; all of them united only in the rejection of the medieval Roman Catholic doctrine of transubstantiation. At present these theological differences have become so subtle that one must be a philosopher with a better-than-average education in order to recognize them in their variety of types. If our salvation depended up such a recognition, then the Kingdom of Heaven would be accessible only to learned thinkers—which is obviously contrary to the conception held by Jesus himself, and to his own words.

No, what matters in the Holy Supper is something essentially different, something which the shrewdest cannot conceive with all his shrewdness, but which the most simple-minded can well grasp and comprehend. The Lord Jesus announces in this meal his own death, and thus he draws the veil from the mystery of his life's conclusion. And what he himself said at the time about the significance of his death became for his apostles and then for his church the actual core of the Christian faith and of the Christian message; and it has remained so until this day. When Paul wished to condense the contents of his missionary preaching in a single sentence, he wrote: "I determined not to know any thing [namely, in the field of religion] among you, save Jesus Christ, and him crucified" (1 Corinthians 2: 2). And when the Christian Church wishes to give to its faith the shortest and yet the most unmistakable expression, it uses the symbol of the cross. The cross stands over the altars in our churches, greets us on the paths of our homeland, it is the sign of hope on the graves of our beloved. We know only one comfort and one assurance, Jesus Christ the crucified.

The interpretation of his death which the Lord Jesus gives his disciples in the Holy Supper is extremely plain. To understand it there is no need of any philosophy nor of any Biblical learning, but only of an open heart which is ready to see what is here happening, and to hear what is here being said.

The Lord himself breaks the bread, he himself passes the cup: he himself gives up his body and blood. There is therefore no basis to what may have appeared true to a casual bystander, namely, this his life was taken from him against his will. No, he gives it up voluntarily, as a saying of the Lord states in the Gospel of John: "No man taketh it [i.e., my life] from me, but I lay it down of myself" (John 10: 18). But he does not cast it from himself, as may happen in other cases, as something good for nothing, for which one has no further use. He gives the bread and the wine to his disciples to eat and to drink, that they may live thereby. So his death is a gift that should be of advantage to them. Finally however, there arises from this eating and drinking a new kind of communion, the communion of those to whom the Lord grants a share in his self-sacrifice—the eucharistic community. This much the action per se, as we see it taking place before our eyes, tells us.

The Lord Christ, however, adds to the action his explaining words. These words are not transmitted identically in the various accounts, but on the whole the meaning is the same. According to these accounts, as Jesus broke and distributed the bread, he said, "Take, eat: this is my body, which is given for you"; and in passing the cup: "Take and drink all of it; this cup is the new testament in my blood, which will be shed for you and for many for the remission of sins." And both times he added as a conclusion, "This do in remembrance of me."

We are therefore told here that the Lord does not withdraw from us by his death, especially not if we accept his gift. On the contrary, here he would become entirely united with us, here he gives himself fully to us, his body and his blood belong to us—"for you." Nay, in this "for you" lies the real and effective mystery of his death on the cross. For it does not merely say that Jesus dies for his own friends, like a soldier for his people and country, or like the saver of a life who snatches another from the flames or from the waves and perishes himself. He says so: "For you for the remission of sins." This is the unparalleled feature of his death, that he dies in our place, the just for the unjust, the holy one for the sinners. And now we stand in his place: free of all guilt and through him and on his account beloved children of God.

This is the end of the old covenant, in which the relation between God and us was regulated according to the principle of reward and punishment. With the death of Jesus for us, the new covenant, which rests on the forgiveness of sins, has been established, and it removes terror from our own death because another has already allowed our punishment to be executed upon himself. Now the saying is, "Where there is forgiveness of sins, there is also life and bliss."

This interpretation which Jesus himself gives of his death, is, as we noted, plain; but in its wonderfulness incomprehensible and in its depth unfathomable: with brain work we get nowhere here. But where a human heart is in distress because it longs for the assurance of a merciful God, where a conscience is afraid under the pressure of guilt, there the message of the cross and death of the Lord Christ becomes tidings of joy: "For you for the remission of sins." This is no human mental invention, he himself has so said it. And he has given us, his congregation, the covenant meal in order that we may not only hear, but also "taste and see that the Lord is good" (Psalm 34: 8).

"This do in remembrance of me." Thus we celebrate with the Christian Church of all times the meal of the Lord in remembrance of his death, and we hear at the same time his voice, which allots to us his death: "For you—for the remission of sins." And we eat of the bread and drink of the cup and listen to the words, "My body given for you, my blood shed for you." This message does not age, does not lose any of its living strength with the passage of time. For in its need for God and in its longing for Him the human heart remains ever the same. And when all the dead are once forgotten, the death of the Lord Jesus Christ will ever be preached and confessed by his church because there flows the source of its life, and the church will continue to gather around his table and confess thereby its crucified Lord in repentance for its transgression, in gratitude for his love, and in the praise of God for His inconceivable loving-kindness, until—yes, until its Lord will come at the end of time, and with him that Kingdom of God in which all patchwork ceases. There we see him as he is, and there we shall be with him forever.

To this great community of those who proclaim the death of their Lord as a message of joy belong this evening also we, who come here to this table. A small company, everyone of us torn away from his earthly home and from the circle of his dear ones, all of us robbed of freedom and ever uncertain about what the following day or even the following hour will bring. But, despite all this, we are at home. We eat and drink at the table of our heavenly Father and we may be comforted. There is nothing that could tear us away and separate us from Him, since our Lord and Master gave his life for us and for many, indeed even for both of the friends who have gone away from our circle and whom we remember in our intercession, even for our dear ones far away or out there at the fronts, for whom we are anxious. For them also did the Lord die, and with him they and we are well protected.

> We are people washed up by the stream of time on the earth-isle,
> Full of mishaps and full of heartache, 'till home brings us the Saviour.
> The father-home is ever near, though changeable be fates:
> It is the cross on Golgotha, the home for the homeless!

Amen.

EASTER MONDAY
APRIL 2, 1945

> But Mary stood without at the sepulchre weeping: and as she wept, she stooped down, and looked into the sepulchre, and seeth two angels in white sitting, the one at the head, and the other at the feet, where the body of Jesus had lain. And they say unto her Woman, why weepest thou? She saith unto them, Because they have taken away my Lord, and I know not where they have laid him. And when she had thus said, she turned herself back, and saw Jesus standing, and knew not that it was Jesus. Jesus saith unto her, Women, why weepest thou? whom seekest thou? She, supposing him to be the gardener, saith unto him, Sir, if thou have borne him hence, tell me where thou hast laid him, and I will take him away. Jesus saith unto her, Mary. She turned herself, and saith unto him, Rabboni; which is to say, Master. Jesus saith unto her, Touch me not; for I am not yet ascended to my Father: but go to my brethren, and say unto them, I ascend unto my Father, and your Father; and to my God, and your God. Mary Magdalene came and told the disciples that she had seen the Lord, and that he had spoken these things unto her.

> John 20: 11-18

EASTER! Jubilation fills all of Christendom today. "The Lord is risen, he is truly risen!" And it would seem that all creation joins in the joyful shout. The might of winter is broken, anticipations of spring are stirring in the air, new joys of living are eager to break through into the light: "Now everything, everything must change!"

We do not wish to censure this Easter feeling. One may well rejoice also over spring and the return of the rising sap, which will enlarge the buds and soon bring forth blossoms. We should also be grateful that the new bread begins to grow which—may God will it—despite all the distress around us still will support the life of millions of human beings. One thing only should we avoid, if we wish to celebrate Easter right and become glad for the true Easter message and the resurrection of Jesus Christ. We must not be misled by the might of such strains of nature so that we regard the Biblical account of the resurrection of the Lord as a mere allegory for that victory of life over death which we see—or rather think we see—yearly in the spring. This is only a mental short circuit. We know perfectly well that the life that blooms out there must come to grief in death. All we do is to push this thought back from us again and again, and thus we defend ourselves against pessimism which is justified per se but after all is of no use whatsoever.

No, to celebrate Easter right we must listen to the message which God has sent us in His word. This message knows nothing of a universal natural law, according to which life is stronger than death, good is mightier than evil, or other such idealistic dogmas, whatever they may be—in which at any rate no one really believes any more.

When the Easter morning dawned a solitary woman was sitting at the grave of Jesus of Nazareth. She had been there once before, in the darkness of the last night hours, and noticed with horrified astonishment that the grave was opened and the covering stone rolled away. She then hurried back and fetched two of the disciples of Jesus, Peter and John. They immediately ran there but found nothing except an empty tomb. Mary Magdalene came back, following them, and remained there when the others left. She weeps: the empty tomb only increases her sorrow. They have taken away her Lord, and she does not know where the body has been placed. Jesus had been her particular benefactor, he had delivered her soul from the deepest distress: the Evangelist Luke relates that seven demons were driven out of her. No wonder his death struck her like the blow of a club! No wonder the disappearance of the body makes her even more painfully conscious of her utter loneliness! This woman is aware of the truth of the Lord's saying, "In the world ye shall have tribulation" (John 16: 33). She knows that a life without the Lord Christ is unbearable for her, in her feebleness and in her distress. And so she stares into the grave and finds there nothing but dark hopelessness in spite of the shining fingers of the angels, mentioned by the Evangelist, who vainly attempt to concern themselves with her sorrow.

This woman is the very first who experienced the comfort and the joy of the Easter message. To help her is the first task of the Risen One.

This is in fact the only common feature in all the numerous accounts, widely differing in details, of the apparitions of the Risen One: that people who already had a close relationship to the Lord Christ are always involved, that the Easter assurance comes to them while they are in a state of mourning, or fear, or even dismay. The resurrection of the Lord is not a general good news which everyone may appropriate. Whoever thinks he can manage by himself his living and dying; whoever is satisfied with himself and the world, or has settled matters with a compromise, so that nothing can disturb his balance any more—such a one simply lacks the organ of reception, he lacks eyes which are able to see the risen Lord, he lacks ears to hear his voice.

But there is a hope for him who is perplexed because the woe of mankind and his own are burning in his soul; for him who is crushed to the ground by the loneliness, far from God, of this world and of his own being—like this weeping woman or like the disciples in the awareness of their pitiful cowardice and their contemptible ingratitude towards the man to whom they owe their best, their all—

yes, for such people there is hope! For them it may mean something when they are told in the Easter tidings of the resurrection of the Crucified: this Gospel message is for those who labour and are heavy laden—and only for them!

And so it may well be that it was not and is not in vain that God gives us, in our situation, a strong impression that the world is immersed in wickedness, as the Apostle writes; that without His help there remains no possibility for us to dominate our life, be it even at the price of a complete inner hardening—and that would mean only that not we dominated life, but that life dominated us. I repeat it may be that we do not receive these impressions in vain. To the one who has lost the assurance that everything will turn out all right, who mourns in his heart because among us human beings evil triumphs and goodness is crucified, who is on the brink of despair because he can discover nowhere a ray of light which might presage a new and better dawn for us and for the whole of mankind—to such a one the risen Lord is perhaps closer than he himself would suppose, even if he does not see him yet and does not yet recognize his voice.

In any case this is true of the weeping woman of the Gospel. She knows nothing but grief and anguish, she sees nothing but a dark empty tomb, and she has no answer to the question of what is now to become of her without her Lord and Master. And that is why Jesus himself stands behind her without her noticing it. But when she looks around in her searching helplessness and discerns him, she does not recognize him but takes him to be the gardener. Nay, even after he speaks to her and asks about her grief, no light goes on for her but merely a tiny spark of hope that this man may at last tell her what has happened to her beloved departed: "Sir, if thou have borne him hence, tell me where thou hast laid him, and I will take him away."

The peculiar and singular dusk in which this meeting takes place we find also in almost all accounts of Easter appearances. The closest friends and acquaintances have not recognized the Risen One at once, remaining in the dark about whom they had before themselves, until Christ himself told them or gave them to understand who he was. The Emmaus disciples walked and talked with him probably an hour or more, and neither his figure nor his voice betrayed to them who their companion was. And Thomas could not believe that he had the risen Jesus before his eyes until he placed his fingers in the nail marks and his hand in the riven side.

There is also a mystery about his coming and going. He suddenly appears and disappears, and it would even seem that he was seen at various places at the same time.

Under these circumstances it is understandable that it is simply impossible to arrange the various accounts of the Resurrection and of the appearances given by the apostles and the Evangelists into a unit free of contradictions, something that is not at all difficult, for instance, in the case of the history of the Passion. The resurrection of Jesus, in contradistinction to his passion and death, is not what we designate as a "historical event." No unbelieving eye has seen the Risen One, no critical observer has discerned him, and so it is simply excluded that proof be given that the resurrection of the Lord is a fact. It can only be certified through testimony, and thus we may admit it by faith or deny it by unbelief, exactly as the "for you for the remission of sins" by which the Lord has interpreted his death. Thereby God honours our freedom as personal beings: he does not force us and obliges no one to believe and obey, but he leaves us free to decide. If the Resurrection were demonstrable, we should be under the compulsion to acknowledge it willy-nilly, for after a demonstration there is never a "No." We, however, must make our own decision; and to this decision, which remains our quite personal and quite private affair, we are summoned by the self-testimony of Jesus and by the testimony of his disiciples and apostles. This is now our dilemma: to believe or not to believe.

This is how we must understand the fact that the risen Lord did not make himself known directly but only goes far enough in his self-testimony to let us arrive at a decision by faith.

For the weeping and mourning Mary a single word, addressed to her by Jesus, suffices. He calls her by name: "Mary." Then the woman turns about, for she perceives in this single word everything she needs to hear. "Yes, it is I," says this voice. "I know you and have not abandoned you. True, I was dead, but death could not separate me from you and you from me. I am here as the living one and I do not leave you in the lurch. My hand will still hold you and guide you, so that all the demons cannot get at you. For you are and remain mine. Do you believe this for my sake? Do you believe in me?"

And Mary answers, likewise with a single word, "Rabboni"—"my Master." And in that one word lies her whole confession of faith. "Yes, certainly, I believe you, I believe your promise. You have overcome death and are the Living One forever. You are close to me and you will lead me, and no one can tear me away from your hand. I was foolish when I mourned and wept and sought the Living One among the dead. I was blind and deaf, but now I know and believe that my Saviour lives, that you live!" So Mary, before anyone else, arrives at the faith in the Risen One.

The circumstances under which we are called to a faith decision are varied and manifold, like human life in general. God leads every one of us, each by his particular way, to make our heart sensitive to His call: the one into the quiet of illness, the other into the solitude of imprisonment; the one to a grave, the other to the smoking ruins of his earthly property. But always the Lord Christ stands behind us when we look around for help and comfort, and he calls us by our name as he did Mary and reminds us that he is not a stranger: "Have you forgotten me—and yet you have been baptized in my name? I am the one who offered up his life on the cross, and lo! I am the Living One, the same yesterday, today, and through all eternity. I speak to you now and here, and I wish to lead you on the right way. Now is the decision before you. Will you let yourself be led, chastised, instructed, warned, allured, and comforted by me? Or do you wish to be your own Lord and God? This, however, you should know: for you I gave up my life and for you I am here as the living one."

We may freely decline to follow this call, we are not forced. We may answer, "You are only a myth, and in reality dead for two thousand years. I prefer to go my own way." Then, however, we must see how far and to what place we go. It is our own, wholly personal, decision, which no one can take from us, whether we truly can and may speak thus or whether we must not rather confess, "Yes, Lord, I know it; your word is true, and the way in which you lead me is the right one. Forgive me for having sought and trodden my own ways, and take my life again into your hands, Rabboni, my Master, my Lord, and my God." If this pours forth out of our hearts, if we must speak thus, then we believe in the Lord Jesus Christ as the one who not only was crucified for us, but was also raised for us. But if we decide otherwise and turn from him to ourselves, then it is altogether unimportant whether we believe that Jesus was raised from the dead, or whether we believe that his body was somehow removed. In that case, these are only matters of opinion, which do not lead to any personal decision in regard to ourselves and our lives.

The risen Lord meets us in his word and in his sacrament: there he appears before us and lets us hear his voice, there he makes himself known as the Living One—and yet he remains at the same time veiled so that we do not see him and recognize him directly, but can only find him in our faith. It is therefore easily understood that at times—and occasionally in hours of great distress and trial—we should desire something more firm and more certain. We should like to see his countenance, how it is, and feel the hand that guides us, in our own hand.

Something of the sort Mary Magdalene seems also to feel when she recognizes in the supposed gardener her Lord and Master: she wishes to rush upon him, to embrace his knees, she wishes to persuade herself that no doubt is now possible, that it really is Jesus and that she does not behold an illusion of her pining heart. But she does not even have the chance of taking a step forward. The Lord forbids it to her: "Touch me not." A singular saying, when we remember that the same Lord, according to the same Evangelist, fulfilled a similar wish of his disciple Thomas, indeed he actually urged him: "Reach hither thy finger, and behold my hands; and reach hither thy hand, and thrust it into my side" (John 20: 27). Similar is what we read in Luke concerning the first appearance of Jesus before the assembled disciples: in their terror they think they are seeing a ghost, so he says to them: "Behold my hands and my feet that it is I myself: handle me, and see; for a spirit hath not flesh and bones as ye see me have" (Luke 24: 39).

The Lord Christ deals with people individually when he places a person before the faith problem. He does not ascribe to anyone more than he is able to accomplish; but he does not give anyone more than is good and healthy for him. For Mary the single word suffices; from now on the might of her love will retain the memory of this single meeting and thereby also the faith. Thomas, the honest doubter, faces a harder road and receives therefore greater help, and likewise the frightened company of the disciples who, in terror of the Jews, dare only to gather behind closed doors. But at last all of them are completely restored to faith, none of them retains palpable and obvious evidence of the resurrection of the Lord. The appearances cease, the Lord Christ returns home to his heavenly Father, and only for the time of his return in power and glory are his believers promised the complete union with him, when believing becomes seeing, hope is changed into fulfillment, and love remains unaltered through all eternity.

This "Touch me not," which Jesus spoke to Mary Magdalene, is also valid for us. We do not receive a palpable assurance that our Saviour lives, and we cannot reckon with bodily appearances of the Risen One. We are made to rely exclusively on faith, and we find our Lord only in the veiled revelation of his word and his sacrament. The Lord gives us no more than is good for us. But we must also be certain that he does not ascribe to us more than we can bear.

So there ever remains in our faith a longing and a hope which direct us forward and upward. But our longing is without fear and our hope without doubt. The Risen One salutes us, the believers, as his brothers; and he allows us to proclaim his heavenly Father, to whom he returns, as our Father. And this is the fruit of his dying and of his resurrection: a way is opened before us, a way out from this terrestrial world of sin and death, a way into the eternal divine world of peace and life. "Go to my brethren, and say unto them, I ascend unto my Father, and your Father; and to my God, and your God" (John 20: 17).

With this commission Mary Magdalene returns home to the disciples. She does not try to postpone the moment of leave-taking. She knows that the Lord is close to her whenever she has need of him, even if her eyes cannot see him. Her tears have been dried, her mourning has been changed into a lasting joy, and so she becomes the first announcer of the resurrection: "Mary Magdalene came and told the disciples that she had seen the Lord, and that he had spoken these things unto her" (John 20: 18).

Yes, the Easter message is not a Gospel for everybody. First of all, and fundamentally, it is an entirely personal question to everyone in our midst: "Do you seek the man who on Good Friday expired on the cross? Do you need him in order to find peace for your troubled heart? Then be comforted: he is not lying in the tomb, his tomb is empty. He, however, lives, and is near unto you. He would be your Lord and Master, your Saviour and King, if you believe in him. He is risen!"

But this message does not remain hidden; it is passed on, and wherever its proclamation finds faith, open ears, and receptive hearts, there the church of this living Lord arises and carries farther the joyful shout, "The Lord is risen!" And this church knows that the Lord Christ, whose rule is now heavenly and hidden from the earth, will truly come in order to renew everything: "Behold, I make all things new."

The spring outside and everything that is still beautiful and alive in this world of death becomes for us, who know the Risen One, an allegory indicating that our Lord is alive and that because of him we have a glad and living hope.

> Thou wilt complete Thy glorious work,
> Who art Saviour and Judge of the worlds;
> Thou wilt turn the anguish of mankind,
> Though dark be Thy way now, O Holy One.
> Hence Faith ceases not Thee to beseech,
> For Thy deeds surpass our entreaty and understanding!
>   Amen.

Date Due